This book belongs to

Color and Trace

1

1 1 1 1 1
1

ONE

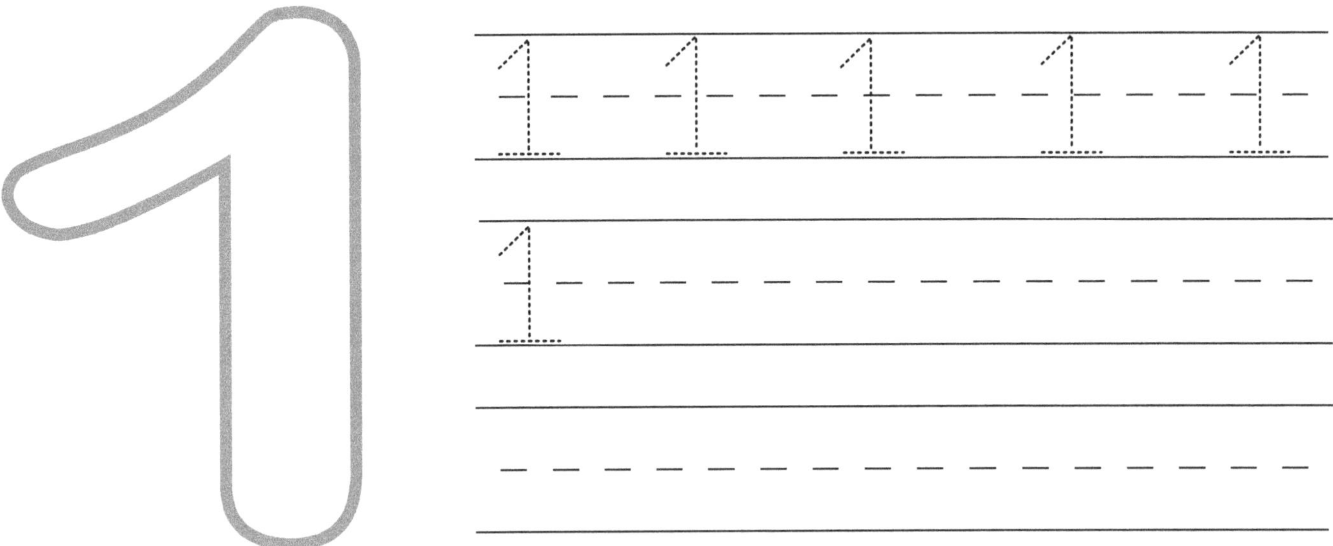

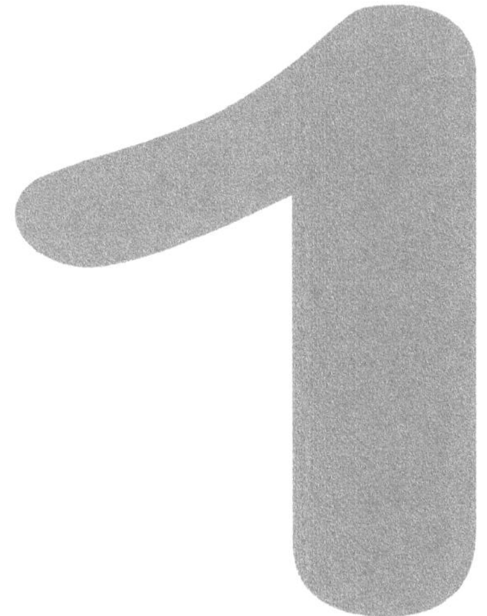

One

Circle 1 Lion.

Color in all the number 1's.

2 8 4 1 5 7 1 10 6 3 2 9 1 8 6 4

2

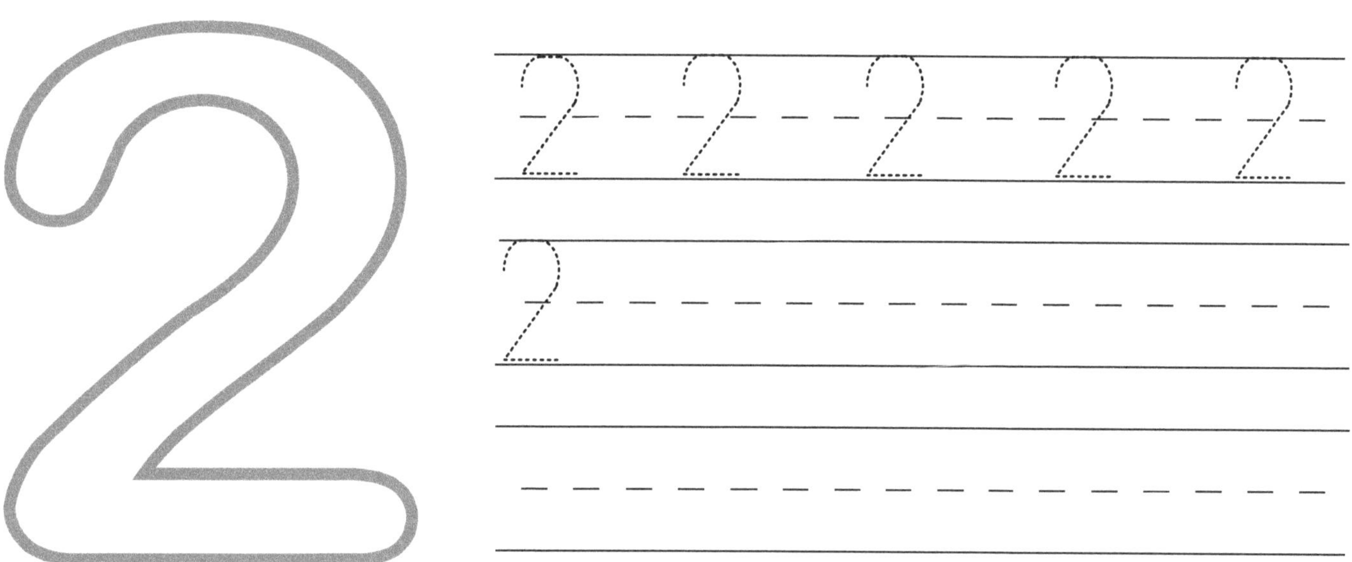

TWO

2 Two

Circle 2 Cars.

Color in all the number 2's.

1 0 2

1?

 **How many animals?**

1

2

Draw 2 spots on the butterfly then color it in.

3

3 3 3 3 3

3

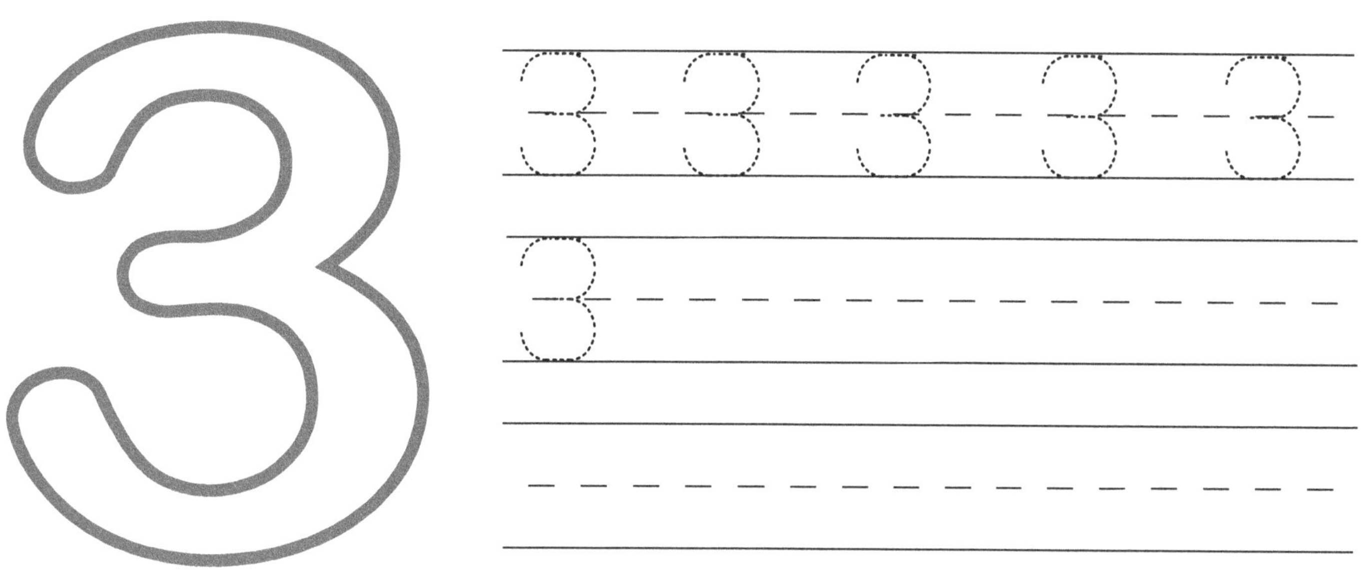

THREE

3 Three

Circle 3 Bees.

Color in all the number 3's.

2 3 10
5 7 5
1 8
3 9 2
1 10
7 3
6

Color and Trace

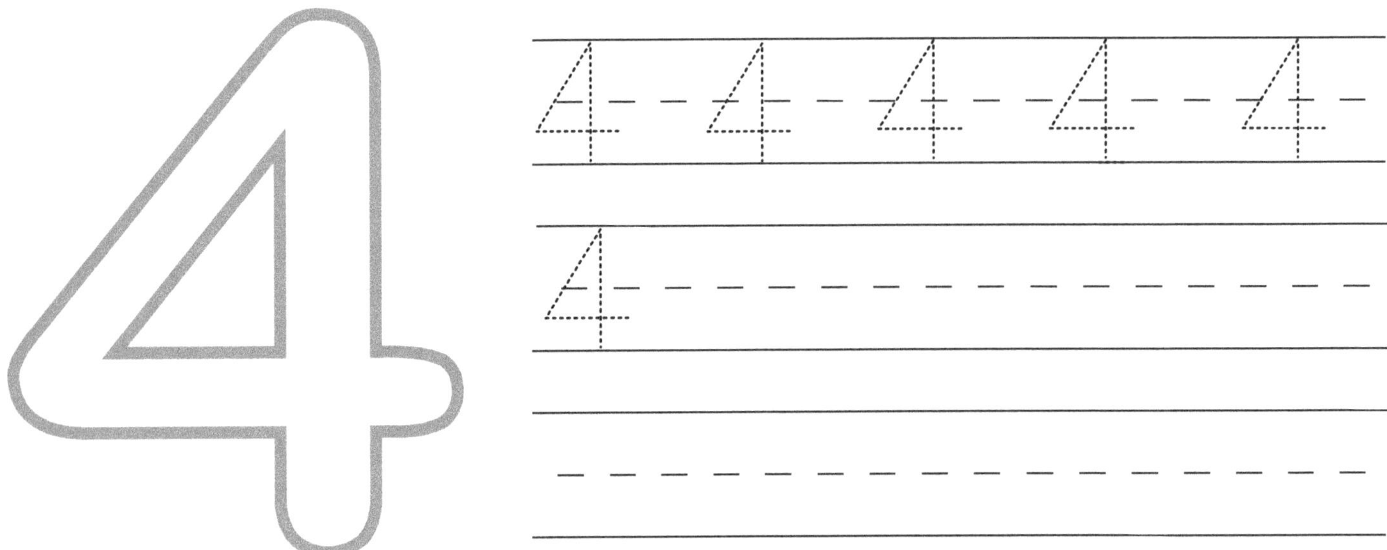

FOUR

4 Four

Circle 4 Dogs.

Color in all the number 4's.

4 2 7 3
2
1 8
5 6
3 1 0 4
4 6 5

Addition

$$3 + 1 =$$

$$1 + 2 =$$

$$2 + 2 =$$

Subtraction

$4 - 2 =$

$2 - 1 =$

$4 - 3 =$

 **How many insects?**

1   

2   

3     

4   

Draw 3 spots on the ladybug then color it in.

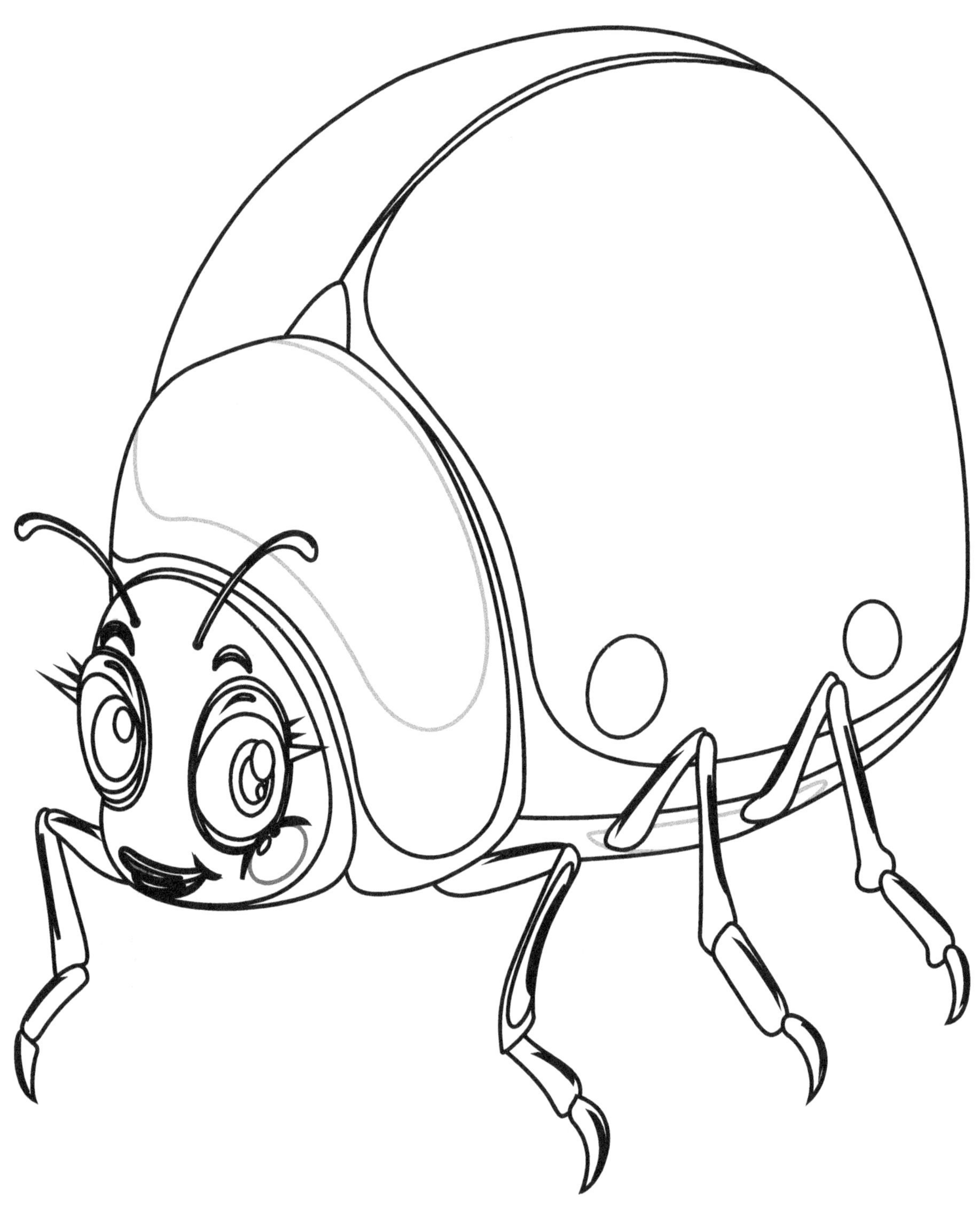

5

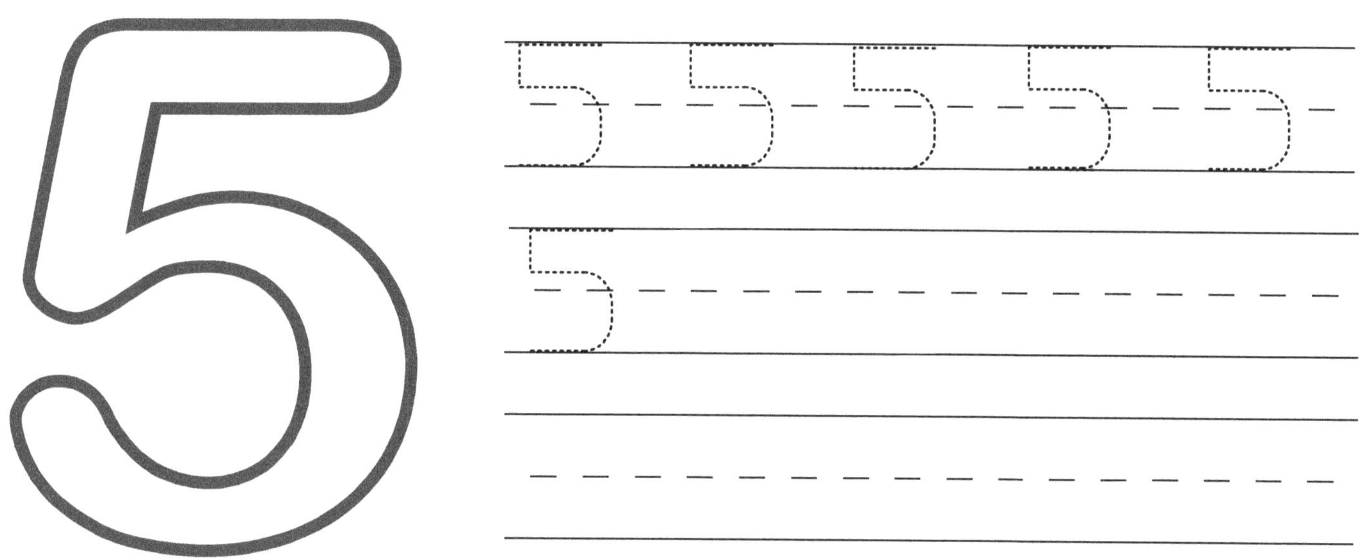

FIVE

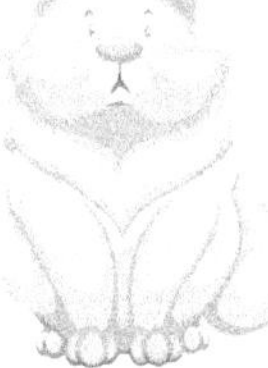

5 Five

Circle 5 Mouses.

Color in all the number 5's.

Color and Trace

6 6 6 6 6

6

SIX

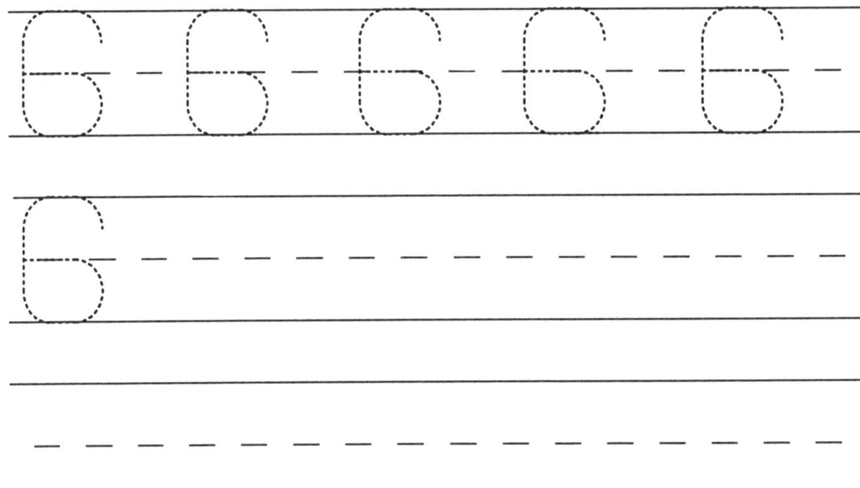

Circle 6 Robots.

Color in all the number 6's.

8 3 6

6 5 2

3 7 1 9

3 1 0 8

3 5 2

Subtraction

6 - 4 =

5 - 1 =

4 - 3 =

Addition

5 + 1 =

3 + 2 =

4 + 2 =

4 2 5

4?

 How many cars?

1

3

6

4

7

SEVEN

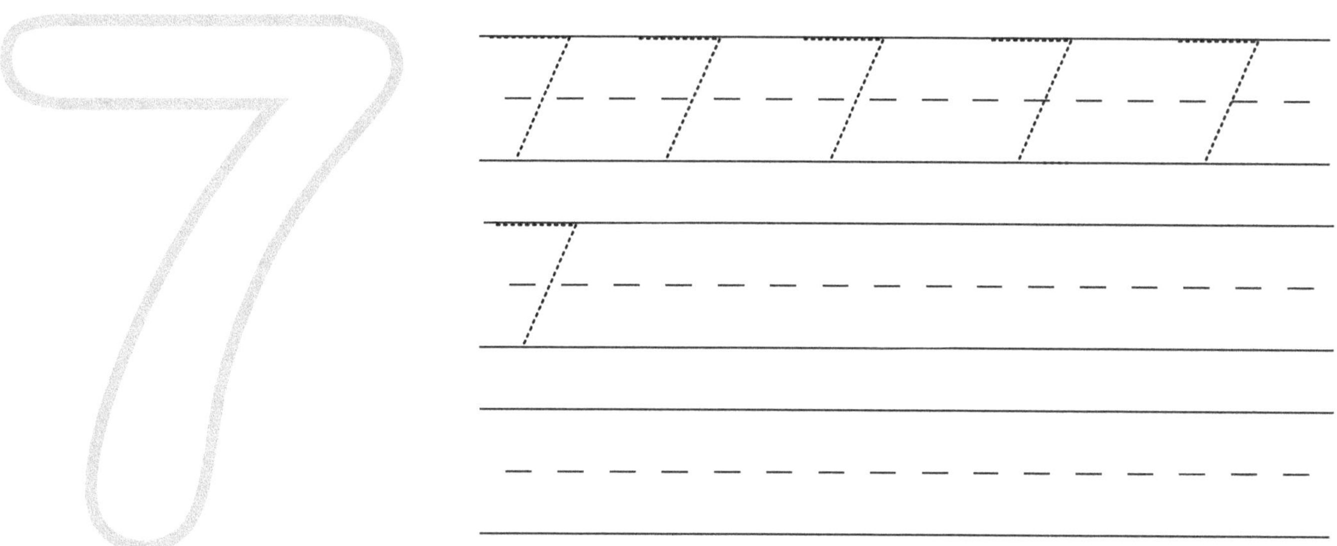

Circle 7 Turtles.

Color in all the number 7's.

5 3 10
6 7 2
8
1
2 9 2
7
6 3 5

Color and Trace

8

8 8 8 8 8

8

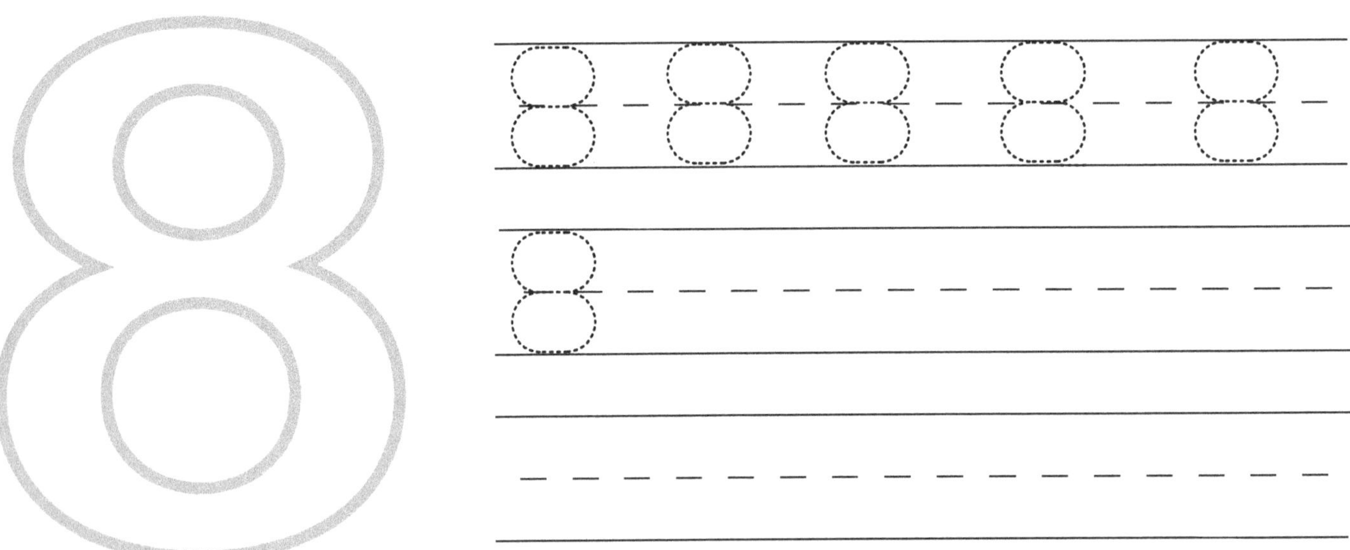

EIGHT

Circle 8 Hens.

Color in all the number 8's.

8 7 6
6 10 3
3 2 1 9
3 10 3
8 5 2

Draw 4 spots on the caterpillar then color it in.

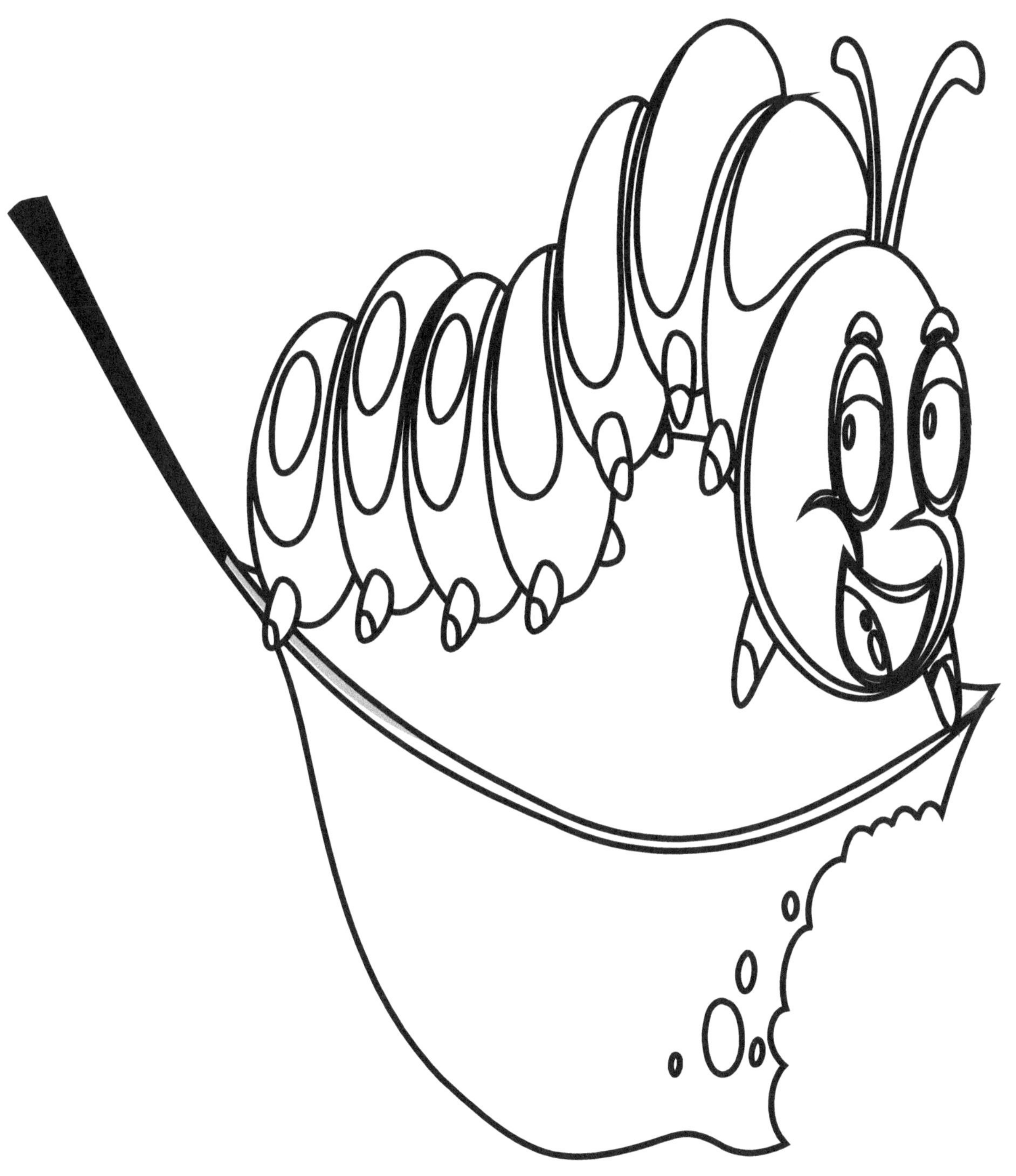

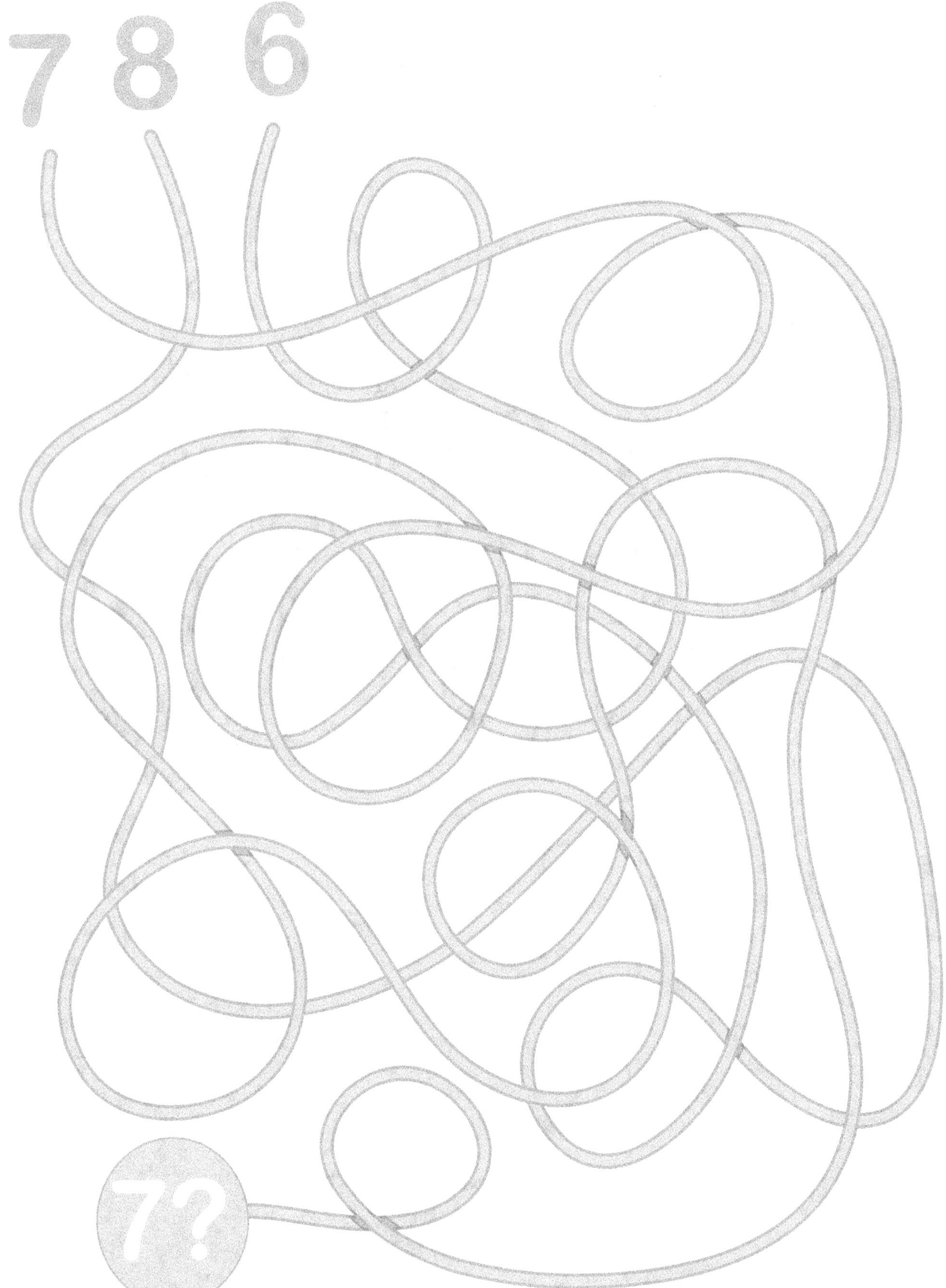

7 8 6
7?

Addition

6 + 2 =

3 + 4 =

1 + 1 =

Subtraction

7 - 3 =

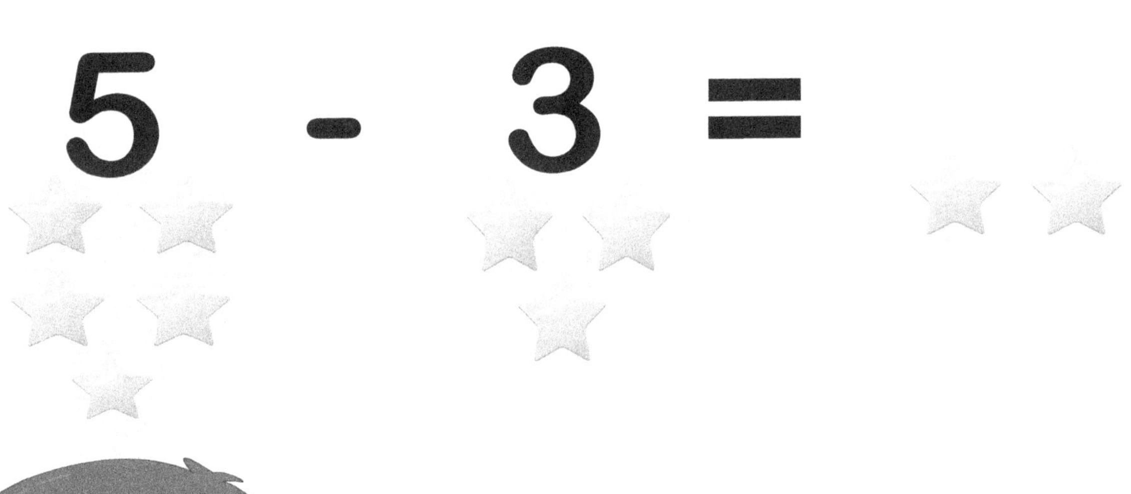

8 - 2 =

5 - 3 =

Color and Trace

9

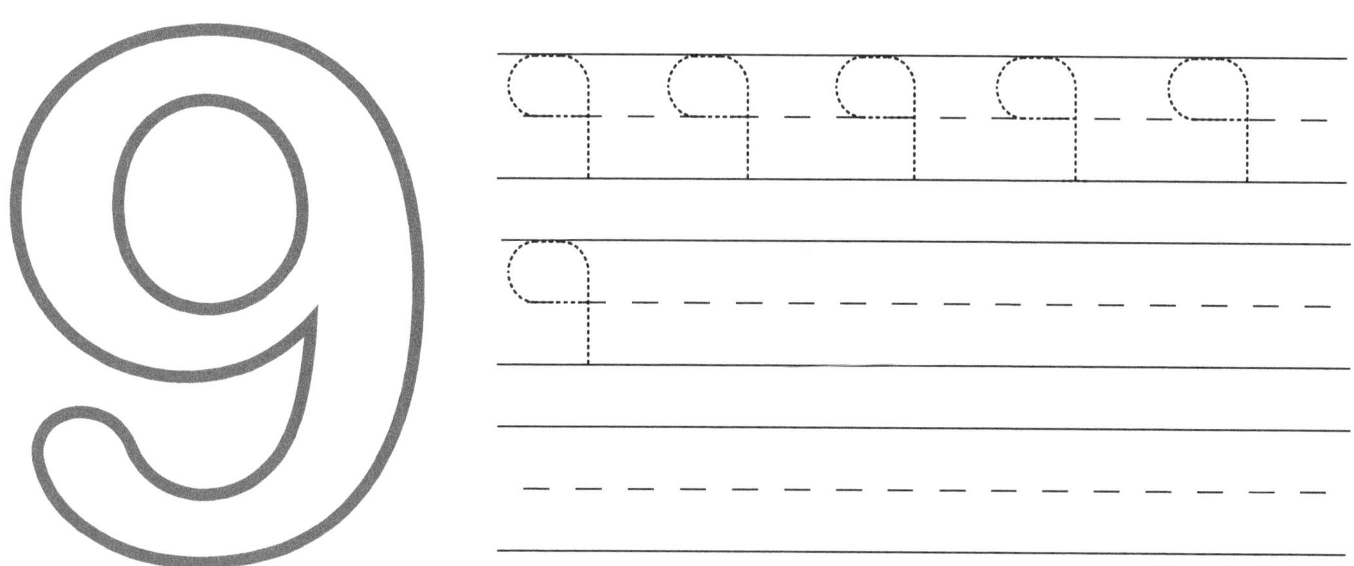

NINE

9 Nine

Circle 9 Elephants.

Color in all the number 9's.

9 7 5

6 1 0 3

8 1 9

3

3 1 0 3

8

6 2

10

10 10 10 10 10

10

TEN

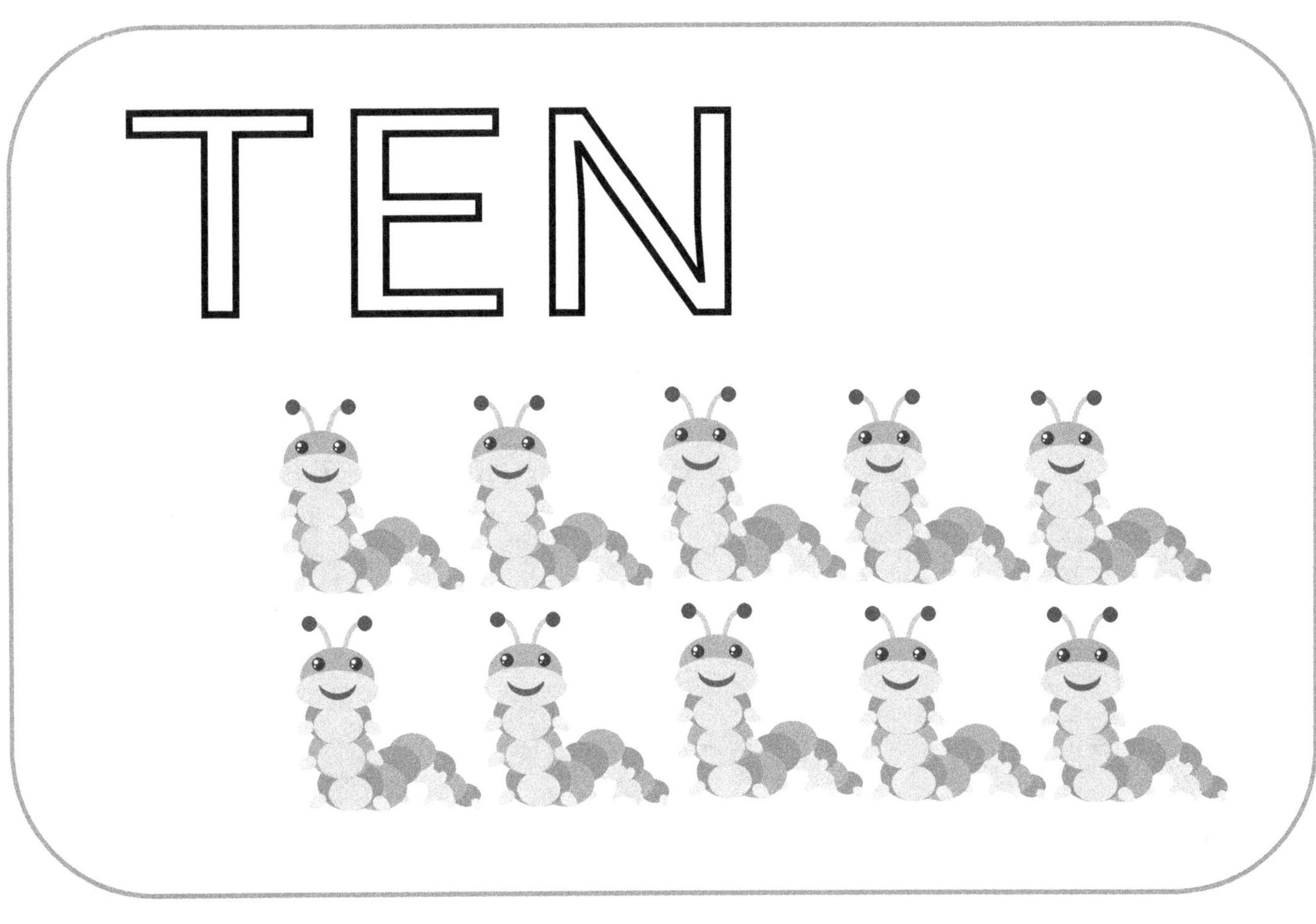

10 Ten

Circle 10 Ducks.

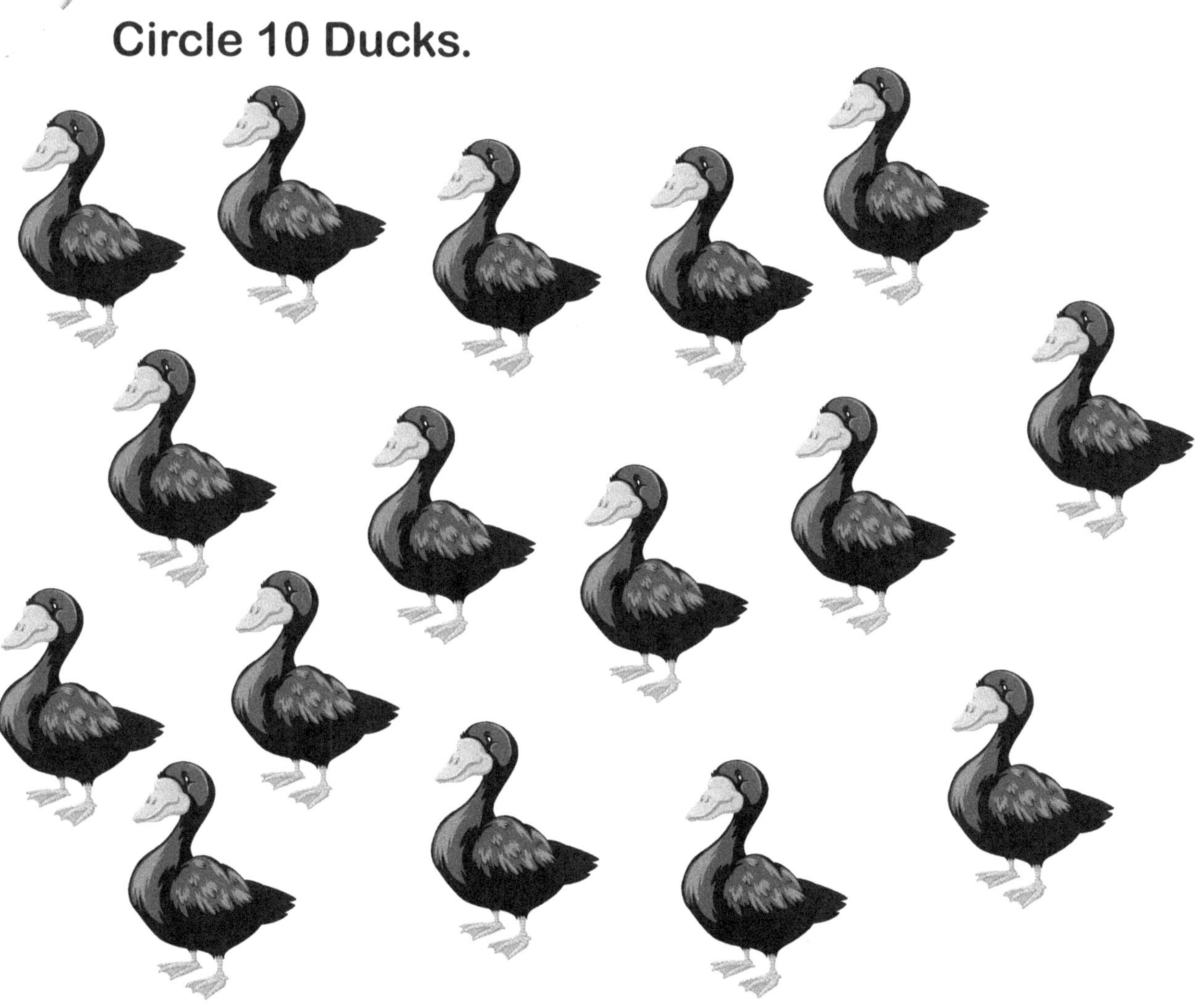

Color in all the number 10's.

10 7 6

6 3 9

3 2 1 3

8 8 10

5 2

Subtraction

10 - 3 =

6 - 5 =

8 - 4 =

Addition

$$9 + 1 =$$

$$5 + 3 =$$

$$6 + 3 =$$

How many birds?

10

7

8

5

5 3 9

5?